IMPERMANENT WAYS

THE CLOSED RAILWAY LINES OF BRITAIN
SPECIAL No 1

THE SOMERSET & DORSET LINE
Commemorating the 50th anniversary of closure: 1966-2016

Jeffery Grayer

www.crecy.co.uk

First published in 2017 by Crécy Publishing

All rights reserved. No part of this book may be reproduced or transmitted in any form or by any means electronic or mechanical, including photocopying, recording or by any information storage without permission from the Publisher in writing. All enquiries should be directed to the Publisher.

© Jeffery Grayer 2017

ISBN 9781909328600

A CIP record for this book is available from the British Library

Printed in Malta by Gutenberg Press

Noodle Books is an imprint of
Crécy Publishing Limited
1a Ringway Trading Estate
Shadowmoss Road
Manchester M22 5LH

www.crecy.co.uk

The majority of the views in this book were taken by the author, but thanks go to George Woods, John Chalcraft, Ben Brooksbank, Tim Chapman, Mark Warburton, David Wigley, Peter Russell and Roger Holmes for permission to use their images. The excerpt from the OS map on page 54 is courtesy of the Ordnance Survey, Crown Copyright.

Front cover **Buffer stop view of the S&D's former northern terminus at Bath Green Park. As early as October 1966 tracks were removed from the station but only as far as the shed entrance as the goods yard was to remain in use until 1972. The bonded warehouse on the right-hand platform retains its British Railways signboard and both bridges over the River Avon are in situ – one was to be removed shortly afterwards.**

Title page **The SDRHT recreated a 'last weekend' atmosphere on 10 and 11 September 2016 when Standard tank No 80072 from the Llangollen Railway assumed the guise of both 80041 and 80043, the locomotives which double-headed the final northbound service from Templecombe to Bath 50 years ago. Is seen here as No 80043 adjacent to the magnificently restored signal box and legendary greenhouse at Midsomer Norton South station.** *Peter Russell*

Below **An S&D cast-iron trespass sign, threatening a penalty of 40/- (£2).**

CONTENTS

Introduction	4	Cole to Blandford Forum	86
Bath to Radstock	6	Last train to Blandford	104
Midsomer Norton to Evercreech Junction	38	Charlton Marshall to Bournemouth West	108
SPOTLIGHT: Evercreech Junction	54	50th anniversary celebrations	120
Evercreech Junction to Burnham	65	Index	127

With Glastonbury Tor in the distance, wrought-iron girder bridge No 268, known as the River Brue aqueduct bridge, still stands today as a reminder that for a few years it carried a through route linking the Bristol Channel and English Channel. This status was to be short-lived, the line reverting to that of a bucolic branch serving the Somerset Levels once the Bath extension from Evercreech over the Mendips opened in 1874.

INTRODUCTION

As 2016 saw the 50th anniversary of the closure of the Somerset & Dorset line, it was felt fitting to dedicate this volume in the 'Impermanent Ways' series to this fondly remembered route. The majority of the images for this book are taken from my first railway book published 11 years ago now, the initial volume in the 'Sabotaged & Defeated' series, which, although reprinted, has been unavailable for some time, so this new edition will hopefully be of interest to readers who have not seen the original book and to new devotees of the S&D. This volume, containing more than 180 images, departs from the original in that it includes more than seventy additional views of the railway, in particular the specials that marked the last weeks. I have also included a feature on the final enthusiasts' special, which ran over the remaining stub of the line from Blandford to Broadstone in November 1968, together with some views of the 50th anniversary celebrations at Midsomer Norton In both March and September, Cole and on the West Somerset Railway. In view of this extra material, this volume has been expanded from the usual 104 pages of the 'Impermanent Ways' series to 128 pages, and some images have been rendered in a larger format here than was possible in the original book.

The layout of this volume follows the traditional north to south coverage of the main line, not forgetting the branch to Highbridge and Burnham. Scenes of an operational railway in its latter days, the specials operating in 1966, freight services remaining following passenger closure, demolition trains, and the ravaged scene in the post-closure years are all geographically juxtaposed to stark effect in this collection. As I said in the Introduction to the original volume published in 2006:

'The images presented here retain a haunting atmospheric quality made poignant by the fact that 40 [now 50] years on from closure they can still stir the emotions of the general railway enthusiast, the S&D admirer and the modeller alike. The very size of the demolition task involved in such a major closure, together with the isolated freight services that ran for some time, meant that it took a number of years before the last remnant of track was removed. This gave plenty of opportunity to capture this fascinating process on film. Although not lucky enough to travel on the line during its operational life, the fact that I was a student at Bristol University from 1967 to 1970 did give me the opportunity to visit the line and to make three memorable journeys upon it: in November 1967 from Radstock to Evercreech Junction and back, secreted in the guard's van of a 'Hymek'-hauled demolition train; the following month from Bason Bridge to Highbridge yard in the cab of another 'Hymek' hauling a milk train; and later while working in Bristol in 1971 courtesy of the S&D Railway Trust when, behind steam, I travelled from Radstock North to Writhlington Colliery.'

INTRODUCTION

In the last half-century great strides have been made at the various preservation sites up and down the old line, attempting to capture something of the spirit of the S&D. 'Sabotaged & Defeated' it might ultimately have been, but it still lives on in the memory of those who knew the line when operational and those who have come to know it in the fifty years since closure. Long may its fame continue to be celebrated!

Jeffery Grayer
December 2016

'Hymek' No D7015 undertakes some shunting at the Evercreech Junction railhead in November 1967. 'Hymeks' were used extensively on track recovery trains during demolition of the line from Blandford northwards to Radstock, and were preferred to the somewhat unreliable North British Type 2 Class 22s that had been used at the start of the demolition contract. By November 1967 the days of the Class 22s on the line were numbered and a combination of 'Hymeks' and Class 08 shunters took over the remaining duties.

The Somerset & Dorset Line

BATH TO RADSTOCK

BR Standard tank No 80039, Stanier 8F No 48444 and Ivatt tank No 41291 are lined up at Bath Green Park on 5 March 1966 on one of the two tracks adjacent to the Midland Railway's stone-built engine shed, having been withdrawn from service a few weeks before. *George Woods*

Right **Stanier 8F 2-8-0 No 48706, with Standard tank No 80043 behind, is prepared for rail tour duty on Green Park shed on 6 March 1966. This was a tour run by the Stephenson Locomotive Society (SLS), making a return trip over the route to Bournemouth and forming the final train to enter Green Park station on the Sunday evening. No 80043 had worked the last up service train into Bath the night before in tandem with No 80041.** *Mark Warburton, courtesy of Mrs Margaret Warburton*

Below right **In its role as Bath pilot, grubby pannier tank No 3681, which has lost its cabside number, draws out the coaching stock of the LCGB special that had arrived from Evercreech Junction, thus releasing the two unmodified 'Bulleid' 'Pacifics', Nos 34006 Bude and 34057 Biggin Hill, on Saturday 5 March 1966. After turning, the 'Pacifics' would leave for Bournemouth, whence 'Merchant Navy' No 35028 Clan Line took the special on to Waterloo. No 3681 had the distinction of being the last ex-GWR locomotive to steam on the Western Region when it was noted in steam on the depot the following Monday, and there are stories that it may even have run down the line collecting equipment from stations following closure.** *Mark Warburton, courtesy of Mrs Margaret Warburton*

Left **It is the turn of No 34057 to be rotated. One of the operational problems of having the turntable located where it was at Bath was that, when used by larger locomotives such as 9Fs and Bulleid 'Pacifics', there was a danger that if they were positioned a little too far forward the leading buffers would foul wagons standing on the adjacent coal stage road as the turntable revolved.** *George Woods*

Below left **Both 'Pacifics' are captured in this view, which shows No 34006 in the process of being turned on the 60-foot table at Green Park shed. This was always a bit of a tight fit as the 'Pacifics' had a wheelbase of 57ft 6in and an overall length of 67ft 4¾in. Southern Region authorities had to check with Bath shed that they had a 60-foot turntable available before allowing a Bulleid 'Pacific' up the line for the first time in March 1951.**

Right **With the DMU that had brought enthusiasts from Birmingham to Bath to travel on the SLS special of 6 March 1966 on the left, Nos 48706 and 80043 make ready for departure to Bournemouth with the SLS headboard attached. The Standard tank was coupled inside to provide steam heating for the carriages. The DMU comprised two three-car Class 101 Metro-Cammell units from Tyseley depot and, ironically for a steam-dominated route, it was to form the last departure from Green Park on the Sunday evening.** *Mark Warburton, courtesy of Mrs Margaret Warburton*

Below right **The overall roof of Bath Green Park, although devoid of glass and badly in need of a coat of paint, still lends the derelict station an air of importance in this autumn 1967 view. In December of that year the City Council made use of the site as a temporary car park before tarmac was laid in 1968 to make the provision more permanent. The signboard remains on the left, although only the outline of the typical LMS sign remains.**

A buffer-stop view of the S&D's former northern terminus. As early as October 1966 tracks were removed from the station, but only as far as the shed entrance, as the goods yard was to remain in use until 1972. The bonded warehouse on the right-hand platform retains its British Railways signboard and both bridges over the River Avon are in situ – one was to be removed shortly afterwards.

The begrimed exterior of Bath Green Park with a selection of 1960s vehicles on display, including a Triumph Herald, Morris Minor, Ford Popular and Mark 1 Cortina. After closure the station lay derelict for sixteen years before being magnificently restored by Sainsburys in 1982.

The triumphant return of a 7F to Green Park on 4/5 March 2006 for the 40th anniversary of the S&D's closure is captured in this nocturnal view of No 53809 standing on a short length of track under the restored trainshed. It went on to be reunited for the first time with the other survivor, No 53808, on the West Somerset Railway (WSR). See page 124 for a 50th anniversary view of this locomotive on the WSR. *Rail Photoprints*

Right The famous grounded coach body used for enginemen's 'Mutual Improvement Classes' resists the tide of destruction engulfing the old Midland shed at Bath. The turntable was cut up as early as October 1966. The shattered remains of the S&D wooden engine shed lie mangled and twisted on the left. Running lines still remain on the right, as goods traffic continued to be handled in Midland Bridge Yard until June 1971, after which large numbers of condemned box vans were held here for the next twelve months or so – the final working out of Bath being in April 1972.

Below right Seen from the S&D tracks in the foreground in August 1964, a green-liveried Brush Type 4 passes Bath Junction with the 1.55pm goods service from Green Park to Bristol via Mangotsfield, on this day consisting of three vehicles. While main-line diesels were by this date regular visitors to Bath on the Midland route from Mangotsfield, they never worked on the S&D until after closure, although the occasional DMU did venture south from Bath. One of the gasholders of the nearby gasworks is a prominent feature in this view; the last of these structures was not demolished until 2014 as part of the £400m Riverside redevelopment of the city. Bath was one of the first cities in the UK to manufacture its own town gas, with the local gasworks closing in mid-1971 when conversion to natural gas took place.

Above left Looking north-west from the entrance to Devonshire Tunnel in late 1967 the long straight stretch down the 1 in 50 grade to Bath Junction can be seen. This has now been converted into a linear park and, although the deep cutting in the foreground was later infilled together with much backfilling to seal the tunnel mouth, this was re-excavated and opened to pedestrians and cyclists as part of the Two Tunnels project, together with Combe Down Tunnel, in April 2013.

Below left Lyncombe Vale was a pleasant spot between Devonshire and Combe Down tunnels, no doubt giving a welcome, if brief, respite and fresh air to locomotive crews. Track has only just been recovered in this spring 1968 view, the sleepers and chairs awaiting removal.

While in the vicinity of the northern portal of Combe Down Tunnel, I could hear the unmistakable throb of diesel engines deep within the confines of the bore. A few minutes later a Class 08 shunter emerged into the daylight. Expecting to see a train of wagons being towed, the sight that met my eyes was rather surprising, as there were only a few lengths of rail chained to the rear drawbar and gouging out the sleepers as they were dragged unceremoniously down the grade to Bath Junction. This can hardly have been an economic method of recovery, but in view of the restrictions of the tunnel this was the easiest way to manhandle lengths of rail in such a confined space. However, it was a good job the sleepers didn't have to put up with much of this treatment.

The Somerset & Dorset Line

It is late October 1967 and the autumn tints are beginning to show in the trackside foliage as the line exits the southern portal of the mile-long Combe Down Tunnel. Track recovery was to reach this spot by the turn of the year.

BATH TO RADSTOCK

Right Literally the end of the line, as track recovery makes its inexorable way north of Midford goods yard, leaving just the sleepers and chairs to be reclaimed on this section. The cant and curvature of the alignment are typical of this stretch of the Bath extension, only single track being affordable between Midford and Bath Junction due to the difficult nature of the terrain.

Below right The gaunt shell of Midford box still stands in October 1967, while the station building has already suffered at the hands of the demolition gangs, whose bottles of propane gas can be seen at the platform end. The tablet-catching apparatus leans drunkenly against the wall of the box.

Left **A visit to Midford on 22 October 1967 was to prove very timely, for track removal gangs were to reach the station by the first week in December. If it was not for the film of rust evident on the rails in this signal-top view, there is little to indicate that this is not a working railway. However, soon it would go the way of the Camerton branch, whose remains can be seen passing under the viaduct in the foreground.**

Below left **No doubt Percy Savage and Harry Wiltshire, the two long-serving signalmen at Midford, would turn in their graves to see the state of their once immaculately kept box. The rusting levers stand silent witness to the impending destruction, although fortunately the interior of the box has since been lovingly recreated at Washford on the West Somerset Railway.**

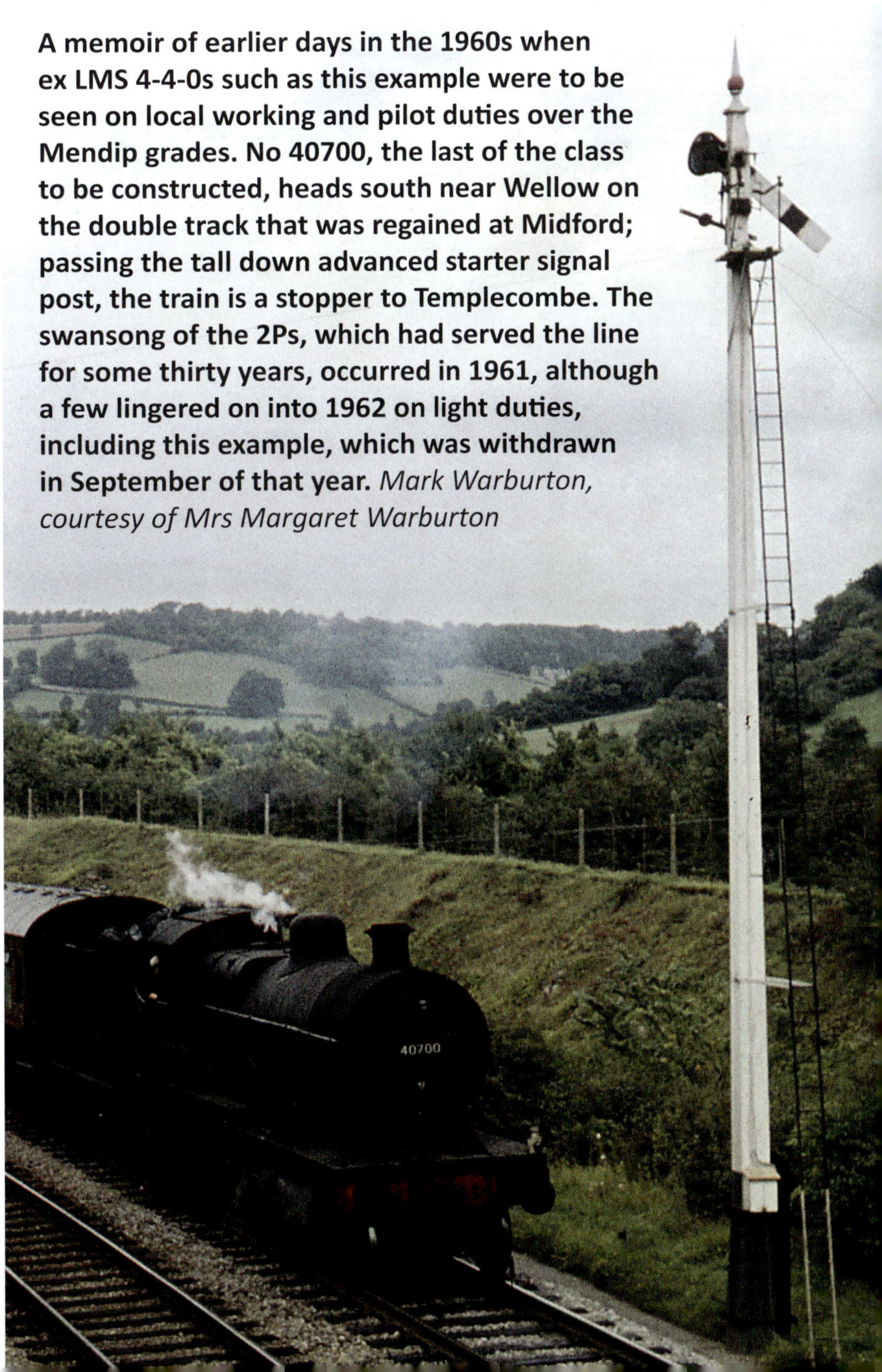

BATH TO RADSTOCK

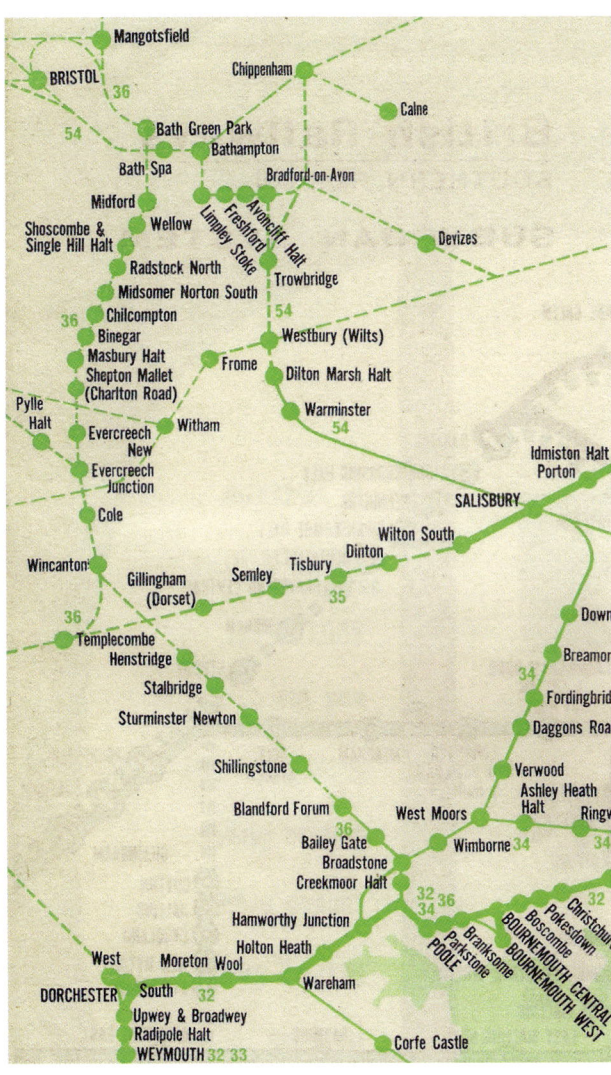

A memoir of earlier days in the 1960s when ex LMS 4-4-0s such as this example were to be seen on local working and pilot duties over the Mendip grades. No 40700, the last of the class to be constructed, heads south near Wellow on the double track that was regained at Midford; passing the tall down advanced starter signal post, the train is a stopper to Templecombe. The swansong of the 2Ps, which had served the line for some thirty years, occurred in 1961, although a few lingered on into 1962 on light duties, including this example, which was withdrawn in September of that year. *Mark Warburton, courtesy of Mrs Margaret Warburton*

The evening sun imparts a golden glow to the stonework of the empty Wellow station building, photographed in November 1967. The signal box is the distance is now the only S&D box to survive in its correct location. It is rumoured that artist Peter Blake, who designed the album cover for Sgt Pepper and converted the house, infilling the space between the platforms to make a sunken garden, entertained the Beatles here on more than one occasion.

BATH TO RADSTOCK

Right Captured from a departing train is this charming period piece at Shoscombe, as a lone female passenger makes her way past the spartan waiting facilities and hut that doubled as a ticket office for this well-patronised halt. What would the inhabitants of this bucolic spot give today for a rail service that could see you in the centre of Bath in 20 minutes?

Below right Shoscombe & Single Hill Halt retains its concrete platforms and signboards in this autumn 1967 view. A separate demolition contract was awarded for the section from Writhlington to Bath Junction, which started in July of that year and was not to finish until May 1968. The isolated position of Shoscombe down steeply graded narrow roads necessitated the use of minibuses as road replacements once trains had been withdrawn.

Bournemouth-based Standard tank No 80138 passes Writhlington box with a Bath train on 3 March 1966, just a couple of days before the end of scheduled services. During this last week enthusiasts were taking every opportunity of riding the few trains that were provided in the period of the derisory 'Emergency Service', which operated from 3 January for the last few weeks of the line's operational life. Access to the local mine was provided by the spur leading off to the left in front of the signal box.

Right With the pithead winding gear of Writhlington Colliery in the background, 'Jinty' No 47276 shunts coal wagons in the loading plant at the mine complex for the final time on 5 March 1966. The last train of coal would leave for Bath behind 8F No 48760 later the same day, after which it was taken out by diesel power via Radstock and the new connection to the North Somerset line. This ex-GWR branch was severed by floods in July 1968, after which Writhlington coal went the long way round via Frome and Westbury. Following cessation of production in September 1973 the last truck of coal left Writhlington in November.

Below right **Bagnall 0-6-0T Cranford** is seen at Writhlington in December 1971 while operating services on one of the open days of the S&D Trust based at Radstock. The Bagnall prepares to couple up to the brake vans for the return trip to Radstock after having run round at Writhlington. The coal wagons on the left testify to the operative nature of the pit here, and BR continued to service this colliery, together with the nearby Kilmersdon mine, until September 1973, thus bringing to an end mining in the North Somerset coalfield.

An unidentified 'Hymek' shunts a rake of coal wagons adjacent to Radstock shed. In the foreground are the abutments of the former Tyning's Arch bridge across the line, which formerly served Tyning Colliery.

Right **This view of Radstock shed, which was a sub-shed of Bath Green Park, shows the three-way point that was removed by members of the S&D Trust in June 1976 for re-use at its subsequent base on the West Somerset Railway at Washford.**

Below right **Looking west, it's a quiet time at Radstock North during the dying days, when the signal box still controlled the level crossing, one of an adjacent pair that caused traffic chaos on many occasions, particularly during busy summer Saturdays. Note the typical fire buckets on the wall of the down-side buildings and the number 38 on the extreme right, denoting the concrete footbridge that crossed the tracks at the Bath end of the platforms.** *Roger Holmes*

Left **The gradient post beneath the station nameboard in this spring 1968 view gives a graphic illustration of the change in grade to 1 in 55 up. The start of the assault on Mendip began at the platform end of Radstock North for southbound trains.**

Below left **From the footbridge vantage point a full load of Writhlington coal is seen heading across Radstock North level crossing to gain access to the spur line to the Bristol & North Somerset line, which it would follow en route to Portishead Power Station.**

The signalman of Radstock West box hands over the token to the driver of the doyen of the 'Hymek' Class, No D7000, in November 1967. The train, conveying coal from Writhlington Colliery, was bound for Portishead Power Station via the North Somerset line over the relatively recent connection with the S&D put in following closure of the latter route. This route only lasted until July 1968 when serious storms and flooding severed the line near Pensford. As this damage was never repaired, it necessitated a much longer trip to Bristol via Frome.

Above **'Hymek'-hauled empties from Portishead via the North Somerset line are held at Radstock North gates awaiting clearance into the station and on to Writhlington Colliery. Although the signal box here was demolished in 1967, the station signboard remains in situ in this February 1968 view.**

Opposite top **The LCGB 'Somerset Quarryman' special of 16 April 1972 negotiates the former S&D level crossing at Radstock North en route to Writhlington. The train had originated at Paddington and was formed of Class 123 set No L713 (Nos 52105/59821/59237/52093). Note the Bristol Omnibus vehicle in its attractive green and cream livery held at the gates.** *John Chalcraft, Rail Photoprints*

Opposite bottom **Following its trip to Writhlington, the special returns to the ex-GWR North Somerset line at Radstock, the new spur to the S&D being visible in the right background. The special went on to visit Merehead Quarry, Cranmore and Ludgershall before returning to Paddington.** *John Chalcraft, Rail Photoprints*

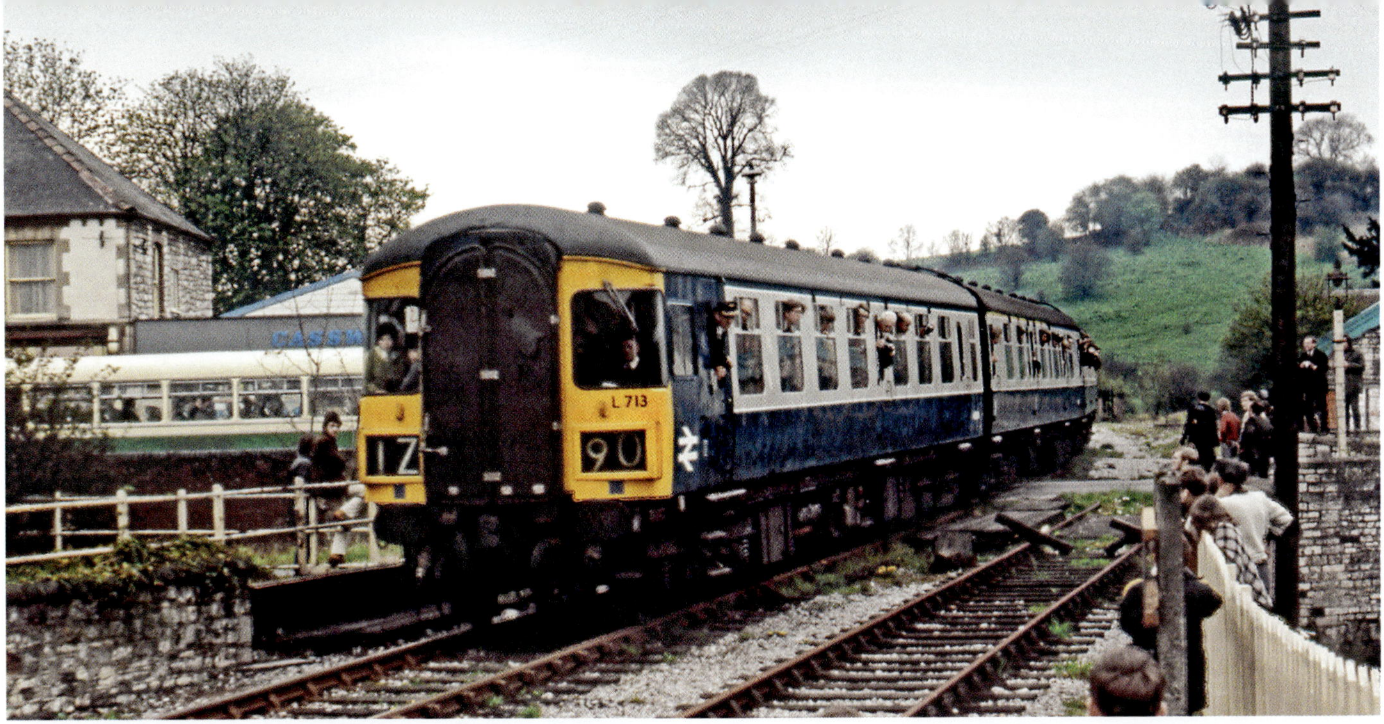
L 713
1Z
90

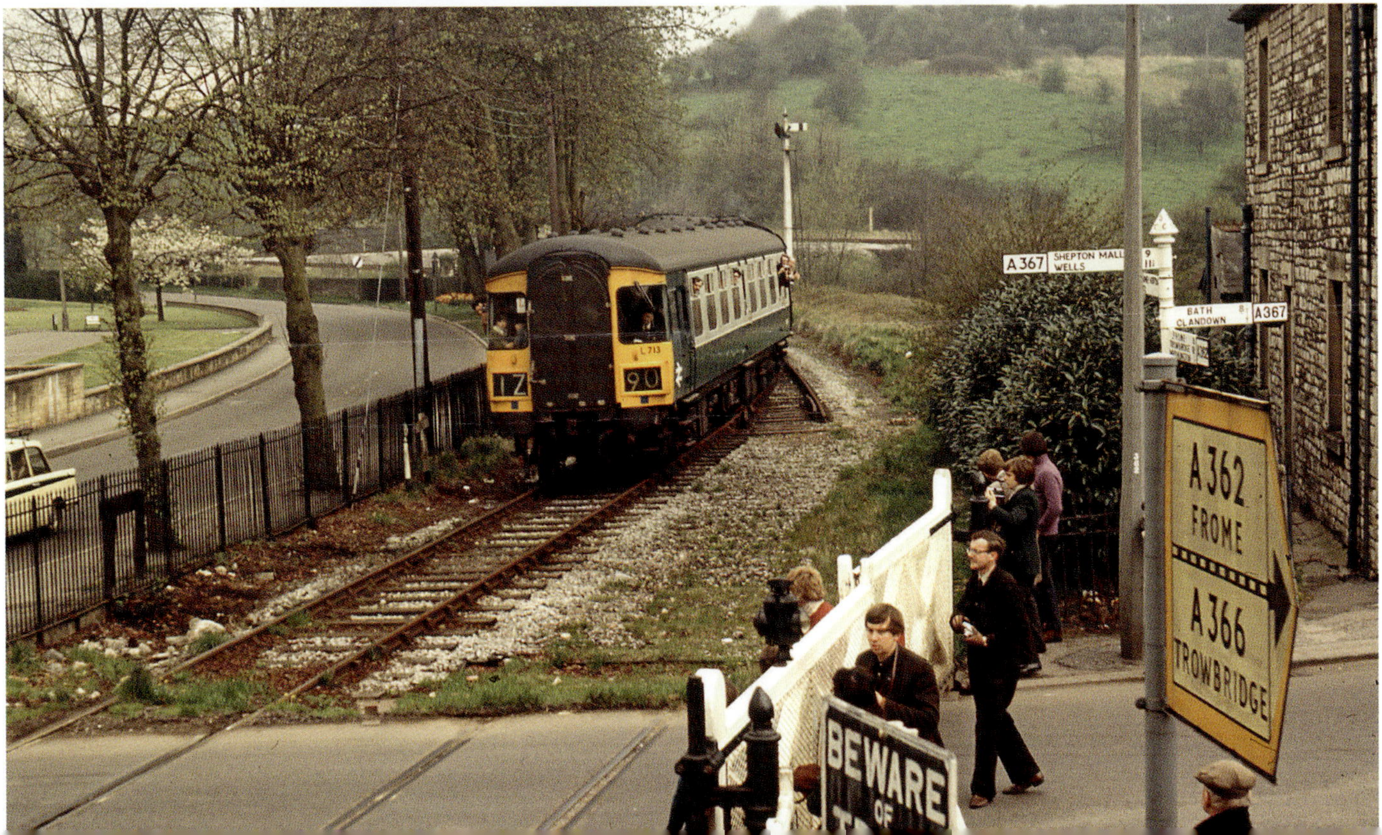
A367
WELLS
BATH
CLANDOWN
A367
A 362
FROME
A 366
TROWBRIDGE
BEWARE

The motorists (and pedestrians) of Radstock no doubt breathed a sigh of relief when passenger services were withdrawn from both stations in the town, as long tailbacks were legendary when one, or worse, both sets of level crossing gates had to be opened for trains. The remaining goods traffic was surely only a minor inconvenience to road users as Class 08 shunter No D3182 leaves the former GWR station with coal empties. Note the remains of the platform-end water crane, now missing its bag.

Radstock West box, situated at the west end of the former GWR station, controlled both the adjacent level crossing over the busy Bath road and, since demolition of the North box, also traffic over the former S&D route. The distinctive roof of the Market Hall is visible in the background. The box was subsequently dismantled and moved in November 1975 to Didcot Railway Centre, where it has since been re-erected.

Left A calendar for November 1967 is on view inside Radstock West box. It was the signalman of this box who kindly arranged for me to travel in the brake van of a demolition train from Radstock to Evercreech Junction during that month.

Below left A pannier tank indulges in some shunting in Radstock West yard. Note the speed restriction board indicating that 'Speed of engines passing over this weighbridge not to exceed 4 miles per hour'. *Roger Holmes*

We take a slight deviation here to provide a glimpse of the incline that brought coal down the hillside from Kilmersdon Colliery to the Frome-Bristol route on the outskirts of Radstock. These two views, taken at the top of the incline, show the arrangements for controlling the descent of loaded and the ascent of empty wagons by means of a brake operated by one of the loco crew. In the second view the resident Peckett locomotive, now preserved on the West Somerset Railway, manoeuvres trucks into position prior to descent. *Both David Wigley*

Above **On Christmas Eve 1971 Bagnall 0-6-0 Cranford No 2 waits by the gates at Radstock North to take a couple of brake vans up the 1½-mile section to Writhlington during a series of pre-Christmas steam days that operated that year. The station has benefited from a coat of paint and is looking quite presentable, the S&D Trust having negotiated with BR to lease it for an annual rental of £100.**

Left **The view looking up the incline. The mine here closed in September 1973, shortly before the only other working pit, at Writhlington, also succumbed.** *Roger Holmes*

Above and top right Steam over Radstock again as the Bagnall saddle tank runs through the station and passes a 4wDM Ruston & Hornsby diesel, parked on one of the sidings that remained, on its way to Writhlington. The engine shed can be seen on the right. The S&D Trust operated at Radstock from 1970 to 1976 when failure to raise the purchase price demanded by BR forced a move to Washford on the West Somerset Railway. Washford is now the home of the Ruston diesel, which in its previous life operated at Bath Gas Works as No 24.

Right With the valuable metal now removed, it is the turn of the sleepers to be recovered at Radstock. *Kevin Robertson*

The Somerset & Dorset Line

MIDSOMER NORTON TO EVERCREECH JUNCTION

Above Midsomer Norton South is still substantially complete, even down to the framework of its legendary greenhouse where the blooms that used to adorn the station were once raised. Track removal did not reach here until July 1968, where it abruptly ceased due to the closure of the North Somerset line by floods and the inability of BR to provide wagons for the contractor. Recovery of the final section from here to Radstock was undertaken by BR on an 'as and when manpower was available' basis during 1969.

Inset 22 August 1959 was a Summer Saturday and the heavy 7.40am from Bradford (Forster Square) had reversed at Bath (departing at 2.50pm) and was due at Bournemouth West at 5.35pm. It needed two large locomotives to tackle the heavy gradients, and passing through Midsomer Norton South is Bulleid 'Light Pacific' No 34048 Crediton piloting BR Standard 5MT 4-6-0 No 73019. *Ben Brooksbank*

The brown and cream BR notice board still proclaims this to be Midsomer Norton South station, but the trains have long gone. This is one of the few S&D stations to survive, and great strides have been made by the S&D Railway Heritage Trust (SDRHT) in restoring buildings, relaying track, re-erecting the signal box and greenhouse and in reinstating occasional services on a short length of track towards Chilcompton.

Left **Perhaps the nadir in the fortunes of Midsomer Norton South is seen here with track infilled between the platforms during its tenure by Somervale Secondary School. This view has now been utterly transformed by the SDRHT.**

Below left **Halted for a photographic stop on their northbound journey at Chilcompton, the two immaculate original 'Bulleid' 'Pacifics' Nos 34006 Bude and 34057 Biggin Hill receive the attention of photographers on the train and at the lineside. This pairing must have been the subject of thousands of photographs as they travelled from Evercreech Junction to Bath and returned south to Bournemouth on 5 March 1966.**
George Woods

Above **Emborough Quarry at Moorewood had its own sidings, which were served by rail until June 1965. In the course of time three large stone-crushing plants were built here to develop the site of an earlier brick and tile works, fuller's earth and ochre also being obtained. Strangely, track still remains behind the gate giving access to the stone-crushing plant but not on the main line, which is seen curving away to the left. The main-line track had been removed by June 1968, but that from the sidings not until early 1969, enabling this shot to be dated to the summer of '68.**

Inset **Littering the site in 1968 are a positively lethal-looking industrial building in danger of imminent collapse together with the remains of an equally venerable rusted lorry cab.**

Left **Binegar, a lonely spot on Mendip serving few houses, awaits its fate in early 1968. Signalling was still intact, as can be seen from the tall home signal beyond the station on the 1 in 50 grind up to Masbury summit. Hard to believe that this is the same busy place that featured as 'Boiland' in a BTF instructional film on Single Line Working made in the 1950s.**

Below left **On 7 May 1968 a 'Hymek' waits in the down platform at Binegar ready to receive, from the nearby Masbury railhead, a demolition train hauled by a Class 08 shunter. The signal levers, like stumps of rotten teeth, can be seen protruding from the remains of the signal box, which has already been partially demolished.**

MIDSOMER NORTON TO EVERCREECH JUNCTION

Right **The 'Hymek' was later joined by the diesel shunter, which had brought materials down from the nearby railhead.**

Below Right **Going back to November 1967, some seven months before the previous views, a 'Hymek' heads north in the encircling mist with a train of recovered sleepers collected from Evercreech Junction, the train passing Binegar 'wrong road'. At this time the station was still reasonably complete with its signal box intact.**

The Somerset & Dorset Line

Above Having passed under Bridge No 70, Masbury Station, a train of recovered materials continues to the summit where the 1 in 50 slog up from Evercreech will be over.

Left Standard 9F 2-10-0 No 92233 approaches Binegar with a Bradford-Bournemouth service on 19 August 1962. © *Dave Cobbe, Rail Photoprints*

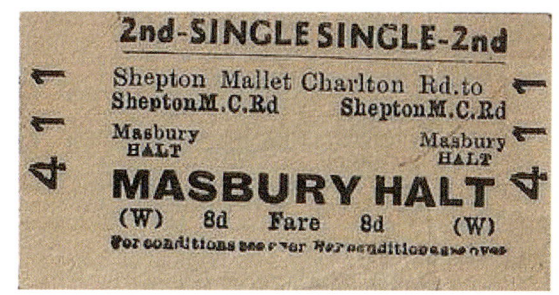

THE SOMERSET & DORSET LINE

This is Masbury station on 22 August 1959, a Summer Saturday when the line was being worked to capacity handling numerous holiday trains. This is the 11.40am Bournemouth West to Cleethorpes train, with a 4F 0-6-0 piloting 'Light Pacific' No 34041 Wilton. *Ben Brooksbank*

Above right **Masbury Halt, where the nearby summit of the line was 811 feet up on Mendip, is seen in early 1968 when both tracks were still extant, albeit that only the former down line was being used by 'Hymek'-hauled recovery trains from Evercreech Junction.**

Right **This view was taken from the guard's van of a recovery train jolting across Charlton Road Viaduct, Shepton Mallet, on a dank November day in 1967. A speed limit of 15mph applied throughout the section of line used by these trains. The outward run from Radstock had been beset by fog, which had begun to clear by Masbury, and visibility was improved by the time Shepton Mallet was reached.**

Left A view of the viaduct from the south on a much sunnier day sees a four-coach local head towards Bath in the early 1960s. *Roger Holmes*

Below left Standard Class 4 No 76027 awaits the 'right away' at Shepton Mallet Charlton Road station with a Bath service. These useful machines were often to be seen on the line; indeed, classmate No 76026 performed on one of the post-closure rail tours that ran down to Blandford in October 1966. *Roger Holmes*

Running in to Shepton a few years earlier is a three-coach train for Templecombe hauled by 4F 0-6-0 No 44560, one of a number of these Armstrong Whitworth machines built for the S&D line in 1922. No 44560 lasted on the S&D until the end of 1964 and was subsequently withdrawn from Gloucester Barnwood shed in 1965. *Roger Holmes*

Returning to the demolition train seen earlier at Binegar, this is the view from the platform of the guard's van as the train grinds northwards through a deserted Shepton Mallet Charlton Road station on 23 November 1967. Note the redundant cattle pens on the left and the water crane still in situ on the down platform.

Right A scene of devastation at Shepton Mallet, where track was recovered in early April 1968. The water tank lies in two halves on the ground behind the footbridge, which was to be demolished shortly afterwards with the signal box and signalling department buildings. The remaining buildings were removed over the next four years, with only the platforms remaining in situ by 1973. These too have since gone and the site swallowed up in the inevitable industrial estate. Charlton Road Viaduct seen in the distance survives to this day in a well-cared-for state.

Right A reminder of happier times at Shepton Mallet's other railway, the former GWR station at the more conveniently located High Street, where pannier tank No 8747 rolls in with 3.28pm service from Witham to Yatton on a glorious summer's day in 1962. The line closed to passengers in September 1963.
Roger Holmes

Left The grass and weeds grow high in the ballast at Evercreech New. Although the cabinet on the right is devoid of S&T equipment, a surprising survivor is the trespass notice, but its dire warnings of financial penalties have a hollow ring and seem irrelevant now. The signal box here had been closed in October 1964 and was demolished soon after.

Below left Recovered sleepers round the curve north of Evercreech Junction in a 'Hymek'-hauled consist on a dismal Saturday in January 1968. Weekend working had been necessary as the contractors had slipped four months behind schedule and penalty payments were looming. Note that the train is travelling 'wrong road' on this section of line due to the state of the other line, one track being sufficient for this traffic.

Right **Passing the burned-out remains of Evercreech Junction North box, this guard's van view shows a recovery train gently easing around the severe curve of the Bath extension in November 1967. The destruction of the box on the evening of Saturday 5 March, after the passage of the last service train and necessitating special working arrangements for the two specials that ran on the following day, remains an enigma to this day, but is testament to the sense of betrayal felt by the loyal staff who had worked the line.**

Below right **The 56-foot turntable at Evercreech Junction is seen here in January 1968 with a 'Hymek' ready to set off northwards in the left distance. It would appear that the table is still operational although, with diesel haulage of the remaining recovery trains, there was no necessity for using its services again.**

THE SOMERSET & DORSET LINE

SPOTLIGHT: EVERCREECH JUNCTION

In each volume we focus on one particularly interesting location. For this volume the junction at Evercreech is featured.

'Hymek' No D7015 runs round at Evercreech Junction in November 1967, having brought in the train of empty wagons seen parked on the down road. It will then collect a full load for its return journey to Radstock.

SPOTLIGHT: EVERCREECH JUNCTION

Right **With services having been withdrawn some sixteen months before this picture was taken in July 1967, the once busy junction at Evercreech now stands silent, although the station is still substantially intact; only the grass-grown tracks indicate that sentence has been passed, the axe has fallen and there will be no reprieve.**

Below right **'Battle of Britain' 'Pacific' No 34057 Biggin Hill takes water at the junction prior to working the LCGB special with No 34006 Bude on 5 March 1966. No 34057 had the honour of being the last locomotive in steam at Templecombe shed on the evening of the following day when it collected a couple of Standard Class 4s, Nos 75072 and 75073, taking them to Blandford for later onward transmission to the scrapyard of Wards at Ringwood.** *Mark Warburton, courtesy of Mrs Margaret Warburton*

Seen from a similar angle to the previous shot, the changes are all too apparent. The tall down starter signal is 'off', but there will be no more trains to benefit from its benevolent indication. The fine water column with its attendant brazier is still in place, as indeed are most of the elements of what might be a functioning railway were it not for the tell-tale growth of vegetation between the rusty tracks. This picture was taken on the last day of SR steam, 9 July 1967.

SPOTLIGHT: EVERCREECH JUNCTION

Right **The perfect country junction station of Evercreech is seen again on a glorious July afternoon in 1967. The centre road, formerly used by Mendip bankers, now plays host to Wickham p.w. gangers' trolley B29W from Radstock. This had been at the junction since February and would remain even after all the track had been lifted, finally being removed by lorry during the summer of 1968.**

Below right **The drowsy calm of a midsummer's day is captured in this picture taken from the classic Evercreech Junction vantage point of the up yard. The p.w. trolley can be seen on the centre road and the track layout is shown to advantage in the absence of any other railway vehicles. What a perfect preservation site this would have made.**

This signal-top bird's-eye view of the physical junction at Evercreech shows the remains of the burned-out North signal box. The curvature of the Bath extension away to the left is readily apparent, contrasting sharply with the straight run in from the Burnham line in the foreground.

Above **Wagons full of recovered sleepers wait at the up platform for onward transhipment, while a guard's van and a couple of empty wagons occupy the central road.**

Below **Six months later, on a very wet February day in 1968, a rake of recovery wagons is parked in the up platform at Evercreech Junction. Judging by the angle of the p.w. trolley it appears to have had an axle removed.**

In happier times, the two 'bulled-up' Bulleid 'Pacifics', Nos 34006 and 34057, await the 'right away' from Evercreech Junction on 5 March 1966. *Mark Warburton, courtesy of Mrs Margaret Warburton*

SPOTLIGHT: EVERCREECH JUNCTION

Sheep in the adjacent field seem bemused to see rail traffic again, which they might have thought had all but vanished. A Class 08 shunter is held at the gates at Evercreech Junction while engaged in marshalling its train of empty wagons. The railhead at this time, January 1968, was at Wyke Champflower, a short distance away to the south.

Left Rail cocks a final snook at road as a Somervale Coaches rail replacement bus service on the Blandford-Glastonbury route is held at the gates at Evercreech Junction while a Class 08 shunter rumbles across with a single brake van. At this time, January 1968, the railhead was not far away and track-lifting would reach the junction the following month. The gates had to be operated manually as by this time the mechanism controlled from the signal box had been disconnected. Two Weymann-bodied ex-Western Welsh Tiger Cubs were the mainstay of the replacement service and JBO 62, outstationed at the Blandford end, is seen here.

Below left The view from the footbridge looking south at Evercreech Junction in January 1968 shows a rake of empty wagons ready for use by the demolition contractors, who were close at hand some 2 miles down the line at this time. The solidly built water tower is a reminder of the workmanship that went into railway infrastructure in those days.

SPOTLIGHT: Evercreech Junction

Right **Demolition is well advanced in this February 1968 view of the up platform. Only the rear wall and chimney breast of the waiting room remain, the signal box and footbridge having already gone. Crossing gates still span the road, which has yet to be resurfaced following removal of the track from the tarmac.**

Below right **With the tracks removed, road resurfaced, and footbridge and signal box demolished, the station is looking very forlorn. Note the crossing gates stacked against the down platform.**

Left **No 34051 Winston Churchill glides through the station past the cast-iron Gents urinal situated on the up platform, which has the additional screening of concrete modesty shuttering.**

Below left **The RCTS special of 2 January 1966, with 'U' Class No 31639 piloting Bulleid 'Pacific' No 34015 Exmouth approaches the level crossing gates prior to a water stop at Evercreech Junction. This should have been the last day of services had it not been for the introduction of the 'Emergency Service' that extended the life of the line for a few more weeks.** *Mark Warburton, courtesy of Mrs Margaret Warburton*

EVERCREECH JUNCTION TO BURNHAM

Track-lifting on the branch began at Evercreech Junction North in February 1967, being undertaken initially by Cohens but from Glastonbury westwards by Wards until Bason Bridge was reached in October. This January 1968 view looking westwards shows that track had been lifted right up to the three-way point, denying any opportunity to use it if required. The small cabin in the right middle distance was for a long time all that remained in the middle of fields to show that this was once a railway junction, but even this has now disappeared.

The first station down the branch was Pylle, seen here dwarfed by its large goods shed and road overbridge in 1968. In 1970 the road bridge was demolished and by the early 1990s the station building had been extended and converted into a dwelling and the goods shed had been transformed into a five-bedroom house. As John Betjeman said at the conclusion of his BBC TV documentary 'Let's Imagine a Branch Line Railway' filmed on the S&D and first transmitted in March 1963: 'I doubt if there is a quieter, sadder sight in Somerset than Pylle when the train has left and it sinks back to silence.'

Above The gates of the aptly named Cemetary (sic) Lane crossing in Glastonbury still hang from their posts, but the ballast stretching away across the levels reveals that the track, originally consisting of two single lines – to Evercreech Junction and the branch to Wells – has already been lifted. Ultimately this location would be swallowed up by the town's relief road.

Previous Page Top Situated between Pylle and West Pennard stations on the 4-mile Pylle bank was lonely Cock Mill crossing. Although one of the gates was subsequently removed for firewood by Glastonbury Festival goers from the nearby Pilton site, this was subsequently replaced courtesy of the festival organisers. The crossing-keeper's house has attracted no new tenants and still lies derelict today.

Previous Page Bottom 'West Pennard station, built of the local limestone,' to quote John Betjeman again as he introduced this delightful spot in his TV film of the S&D. The nameboard still proclaims its location but pram wheels now lie where formerly those of Ivatt tanks and Collett 0-6-0s turned towards the end of the branch's life.

Above **The wooden structure of Glastonbury & Street station did duty as a wood storage area for a timber merchant for a number of years after closure, a role illustrated by this view. Although the station was demolished in 1984, the canopy seen on the right was removed and re-erected in a Glastonbury car park adjacent to the market.**

The LCGB 'Somerset & Dorset Rail Tour' halts at Glastonbury for a 10-minute photographic stop on Saturday 5 March 1966. At this time Templecombe shed still had eight operational Ivatt tanks on its books.
George Woods

EVERCREECH JUNCTION TO BURNHAM

On Saturday 29 January 1972 Glastonbury Town Hall bus and coach stop sees the 13.55 (SO) S&D replacement bus service, operated by Somervale Coaches of Midsomer Norton, waiting to depart, as the destination blind shows, on its 3hr 15min marathon to Blandford Forum via Shepton Mallet, Bruton, Wincanton and Gillingham. I recall that myself and a friend constituted the only passengers as far as Shepton, after which there were never more than five aboard all the way to Wincanton, where we alighted. The vehicle, JBO 124, is an ex-Western Welsh Weymann-bodied Leyland Tiger Cub in far from pristine condition. On the opposite side of the street a Bristol Omnibus MW saloon awaits departure with a Bristol service.

Left **The only intermediate station on the Glastonbury-Wells branch was at Polsham, seen here in the late 1960s. The level crossing gate posts are still apparent, as is the green and cream SR paintwork. The station, sold off after closure as a private house, still performs this function today.**

Below left **The gates at Ashcott & Meare, west of Glastonbury, are wide open to allow vehicular access to the trackbed at this point. A remarkable survivor on the left is the detached Ladies loo – and very draughty it looks!**

Right **The morning after the night before: this is Bason Bridge station looking west towards Highbridge on 7 March 1966. From now on only milk trains would run through here.** *Ben Brooksbank*

Below right **'Hymek' No D7033 arrives at Bason Bridge on 2 December 1967 and the second man alights from the cab to open the level crossing gates to allow access to the Unigate creamery. A few words with the driver secured a cab ride for me on the return trip to Highbridge.**

The Unigate Creamery and sidings, bathed in winter sunshine and situated along the bank of the River Brue, were going full blast in this November 1968 view. Several milk tanks in the sidings in the background are awaiting their turn to be filled prior to their return journey over the remaining stub of the old branch to Highbridge. The creamery continued to be served by rail until October 1972 when the line was severed by construction of the M5 motorway. Unigate sold on the creamery, which was eventually closed in 1987.

Above **With full tanks hitched behind and the crossing gates closed to the railway, No D7033 prepares to move off into the gloom of a winter's afternoon with the return working to Highbridge.**

Below **A brace of Ivatt tanks, Nos 41307 and 41282, run into Highbridge past the shed and signal box just before 2pm with the LCGB rail tour of 5 March 1966.** *Mark Warburton, courtesy of Mrs Margaret Warburton*

A wintry prospect of Highbridge station taken from the footbridge before its present amputation and showing the single line worked as a long siding that enabled milk traffic from Bason Bridge to be handled until 1972.

Right **The famous flat crossing by means of which the S&D crossed the GWR Bristol-Exeter main line at Highbridge station is seen in December 1967. Retention of this crossing, still controlled by the West signal box seen on the left, was necessary to allow milk trains access to the remains of the branch. The crossing lasted until 1971, when a completely new junction from the WR down main line was provided in connection with the terminal constructed to handle flyash used in the construction of the M5 motorway.**

Below right **The 2.20pm to Evercreech Junction on 21 July 1962 is headed by Collett '2251' 0-6-0 No 3215.** *Ben Brooksbank*

Left Seen from one of the S&D platforms, a maroon-liveried 'Warship' flashes across the flat crossing at Highbridge with a West of England train. Trains from Bason Bridge creamery are advised by the notice board on the right to proceed at a somewhat slower pace – 5mph – over the crossing. Highbridge Crossing box, which did not close until March 1972, is still in place, as is the complete footbridge, which in later years was truncated to serve merely the WR platforms to the left of the picture.

Below left Highbridge Locomotive Works closed as long ago as 1930 and, apart from use during the Second World War, lay derelict for many years. In 1970 part of the works was demolished in connection with the flyash contract, and by 1980 the rest had gone.

EVERCREECH JUNCTION TO BURNHAM

The two Ivatt tanks seen earlier come off their train ready to run round in order to return to Evercreech Junction, where two original 'Bulleid' 'Pacifics' would take over for the run up to Bath.
Mark Warburton, courtesy of Mrs Margaret Warburton

Above **With a full head of steam, a respectably clean No 41307 is turned on the 49ft 9in turntable at Highbridge loco prior to returning to Templecombe, having brought in the LCGB special seen earlier.**
George Woods

Right **A side view of the exterior of the erecting shop at Highbridge Works. Only one locomotive was ever constructed here, with two others being assembled from parts – the main task was heavy repairs.**

Above The interior of the former erecting shop seen shortly before demolition. The high-level windows to improve the natural lighting are evident in this view.

Top right 9F No 92243, seemingly with a good head of steam, waits to take the LCGB 'Mendip Merchantman' special of 1 January 1966 on to Bath via the main line to Bristol. However, appearances were deceptive and it subsequently failed at Warmley with a collapsed brick arch. No 48760, waiting to take the special on from Bath Green Park, was duly summoned to assist. *Mark Warburton, courtesy of Mrs Margaret Warburton*

Bottom right With the trackbed of the former line to Burnham-on-Sea evident in the foreground, the two Ivatt tanks propel the coaching stock into Highbridge yard for eventual positioning in the main-line platforms. *Mark Warburton, courtesy of Mrs Margaret Warburton*

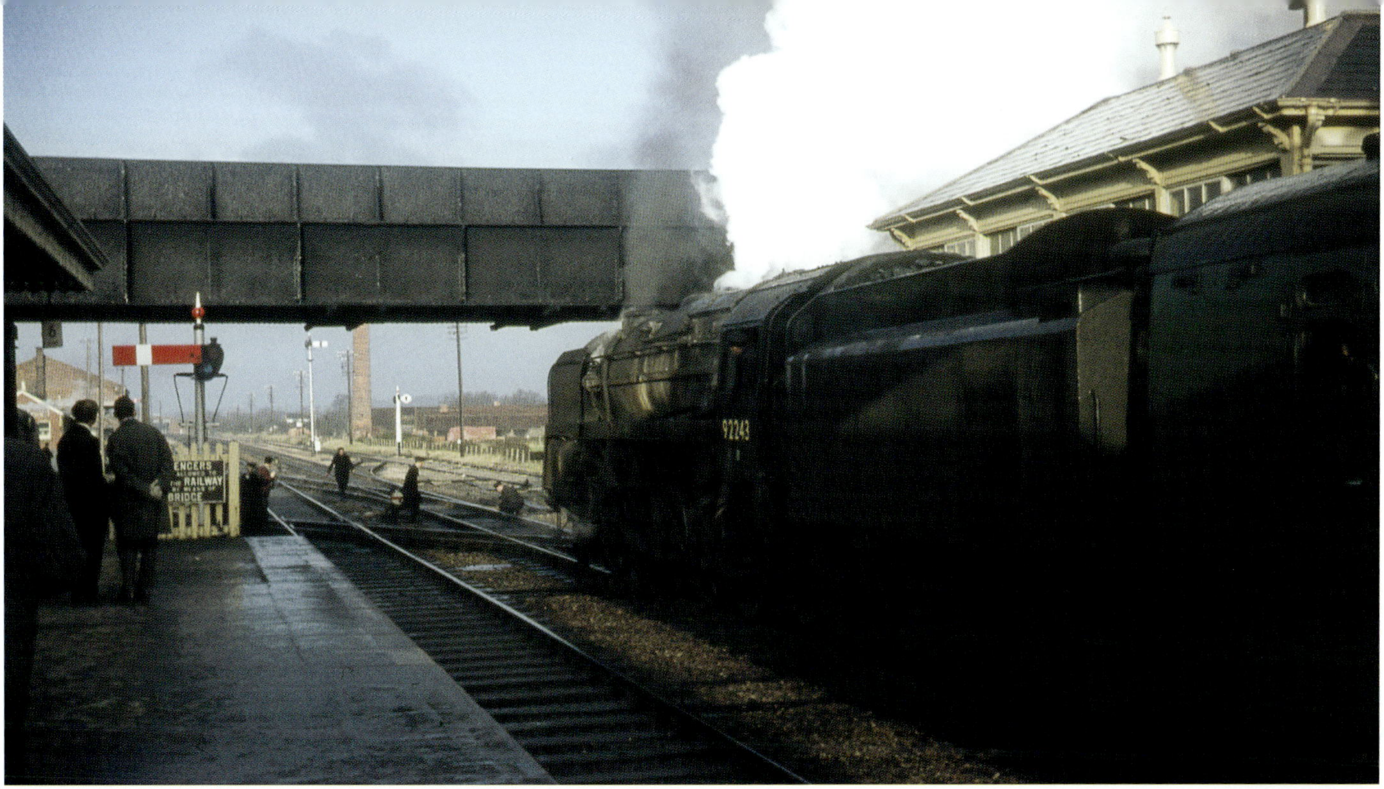
ENGERS
RAILWAY
BRIDGE
92243

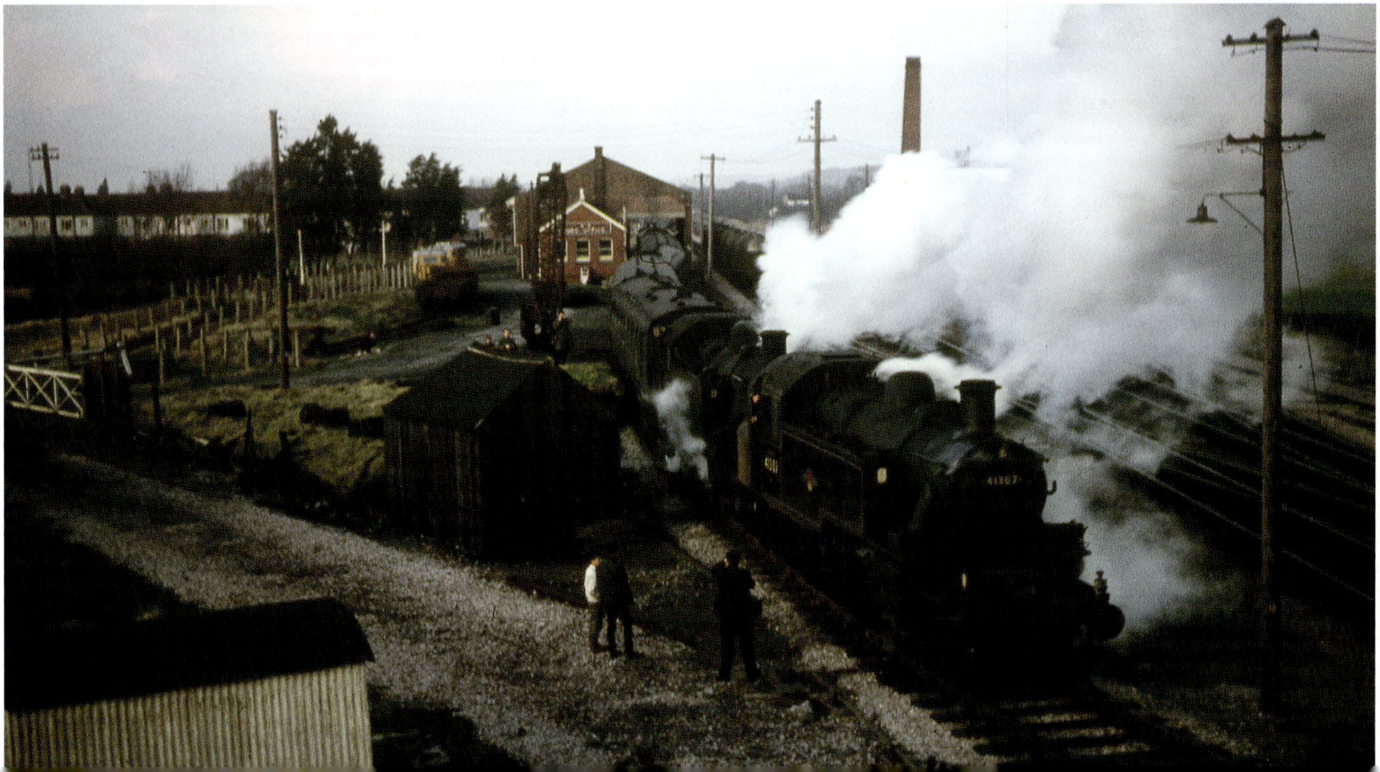

Left This is the scene at Highbridge during construction of the flyash terminal during the spring of 1971. The new connection to the WR main line can be seen in the left foreground and the ramp is taking shape to allow discharge of the ash to the ground some 25 feet below for onward transport by lorries to the motorway construction site a short distance away. In the right background only part of the former works building still stands. The remains of the branch were protected by a new GWR-type signal post, and the BR control office was housed in the wooden hut on the only remaining S&D platform, No 5; the truncated remains of the footbridge can just be glimpsed on the extreme right.

Below left 'Come to Sunny Burnham' would not be appropriate for this December 1967 view of the former terminus. Closed to regular passenger traffic in 1951 with complete closure following in 1963, the excursion platform can still be seen on the left with the main platform on the right now devoid of its overall roof. The level crossing gates leading to the pier are still in place, as is the goods shed. All was to be swept away to provide a relief road into the town. In 2015 a memorial buffer stop was erected on the formation of the line, which extended from the station to a pier whence it was at one time hoped that a thriving trade with Cardiff across the Bristol Channel would develop.

Although Burnham station was closed to regular passenger trains on 29 October 1951, it did see trains at holiday times subsequently, and goods services continued until complete closure came on 20 May 1963. Ex-GWR Collett 0-6-0 No 2204 is on the 1.20pm service from Evercreech Junction on 21 July 1962, especially extended from Highbridge. *Ben Brooksbank*

THE SOMERSET & DORSET LINE

COLE TO BLANDFORD FORUM

This view is looking north towards Cole station through Pitcombe Road Bridge, No 121, a couple of years after track removal. The station building has not yet been converted into a house nor has the housing estate been built on the site of the yard and the main formation. Today this bridge is partially infilled.

Right **Delightful Cole was the meeting place of the Somerset Central and the Dorset Central in 1862. Always a picturesque spot, it still retains a special atmosphere even eighteen months after the last passenger train has gone. A mere four months after this view was taken the demolition gangs had done their work and the scene was transformed forever. Together with Chilcompton and Moorewood, the signal box here had been closed in 1965 prior to the end of services, the box and up platform shelter being demolished at Cole in June 1966.**

Below right **The Somervale Coaches rail replacement bus service is photographed during its generous 10-minute layover at Cole station yard on 29 January 1972. Needless to say there were no passengers waiting to avail themselves of the service on this occasion.**

Left **No more racegoers will throng the staggered platforms at Wincanton. Although looking fairly presentable in this July 1967 view, with signal arm and Southern-style lampshades still undamaged, the growth of vegetation on the permanent way indicates that time has all but run out for this location, which today is covered by housing development.**

Below left **Templecombe No 2 Junction controlled access to the spur to the high-level station, straight ahead, and to the main S&D line to Bournemouth, dipping down on the left to pass under the ex-LSWR main line in the distance, as seen in July 1967. Apart from the odd broken pane of glass, the box is much as it must have appeared on its last day in service, and I recall that there were working timetables and other ephemera scattered over its floor. The box was demolished some four months later.**

Right 71H rather than 82G is how we prefer to remember Templecombe shed, which stands empty and devoid of track in the summer of 1967 thanks to the activities of an advance guard of the demolition crew who cleared the lower yard of all trackwork, although the main line still survived to the right of the shed for a few more weeks. The bridge, under which the long-disused spur used to run to the LSWR main line, can be seen to the left of the goods shed.

Below right The original Dorset Central station at Templecombe stands behind the locomotive shed, both buildings having been incorporated into the former Plessey site, latterly part of Thales Underwater Systems, now occupying this area. The incline of the trackbed from the Bournemouth direction up to No 2 Junction can readily be seen, with the spur on the left leading to the main station at Templecombe Upper. Track removal was completed here by September 1967.

THE SOMERSET & DORSET LINE

Standard Class 3 2-6-2T No 82002 passes Templecombe loco shed as it leaves the Lower Platform with a service from Bournemouth on 4 August 1962. © *Dave Cobbe collection, Rail Photoprints*

Never the most utilised station, Templecombe Lower Platform slumbers in the warm sunshine of the summer of 1967 sandwiched between Bridge 152, Coombe Throop Lane, and Bridge 153, the ex-LSWR main line. In later years only passengers from the 10.00pm train from Bournemouth could alight here, thereby saving the tedious necessity of running to the upper station with the last train of the day. The platform was also occasionally used for crew changes. Apparently it was also used on the odd occasion when a passenger missed a train for Bournemouth from the Upper station, as there was time for them to scoot down to the lower platform if station staff were cooperative and were prepared to arrange for the train to call additionally there. Opened in January 1887, it could only accommodate two coaches. Even when the LSWR station was remodelled in the 1930s, an operationally satisfactory method of connecting the S&D and the LSWR remained unresolved.

The Somerset & Dorset Line

Left **Leaving Templecombe for the south, the S&D ran under the ex-LSWR main line. Looking north, a maroon-liveried 'Warship' speeds its train eastwards through the now closed Templecombe Upper, past the water tower and on to Waterloo. Sleeper indentations can still be seen in the ballast of the line to Bournemouth, track having only been removed a few months prior to this spring 1968 view.**

Below left **The SLS special of 6 March 1966 has arrived at Templecombe Upper at about 12.30 and the tour participants flood across the tracks, obtaining their photographic mementoes in an act of mass trespass that would not be tolerated today, particularly as the starting signal on the down main-line platform is 'off'! The special was drawn back down the spur line to regain the line to Bournemouth by Ivatt tank No 41249.** *Mark Warburton, courtesy of Mrs Margaret Warburton*

Waiting to return down the spur from Templecombe Upper to regain the main line to Bath, Bulleid 'Pacific' No 34042 Dorchester, a regular performer over the S&D, is seen on 8 September 1962, sadly the final day of through services over the route. From 1956 until 1964 No 34042 was based at Bournemouth shed, which helped out with motive power over the S&D on summer Saturdays when many extra services were run. The re-routing of through services at the end of the 1962 summer season was the beginning of the protracted closure of the line. Although Bulleid 'Pacifics' did appear occasionally on service trains after 1962, they were generally only provided in place of a failed Class 4 locomotive, which is all that Bournemouth considered was warranted on the three- or four-coach locals that operated after that date. They were, however, turned out on school and excursion specials, and of course did fittingly appear on the final weekend in March 1966 when Nos 34006 Bude, 34013 Okehampton and 34057 Biggin Hill all graced enthusiasts' specials.

Awaiting the inevitable, Henstridge station is seen in the summer of 1967. At this time the track was being recovered northwards from Sturminster Newton and it was to be only another few weeks before the gangs reached this spot.

The rose-covered rural idyll that was Stalbridge. This July 1967 view shows the rarely photographed contractor's loco that was used for a very short time at the beginning of the main contract for track removal from Blandford to Radstock.

Above A 'Merchant Navy' on the S&D was a rare sight, as they were technically barred from the line due to weight restrictions. However, such considerations were put aside with only a few weeks to go before closure, and No 35011, seen here just south of Stalbridge level crossing, was permitted to run up from Bournemouth to Templecombe with the 1 January 1966 special. *Mark Warburton, courtesy of Mrs Margaret Warburton*

Taken on 16 April 1966, six weeks after closure, this view of Sturminster Newton reveals all the infrastructure of an apparently operational railway still in place. It provides a particularly good view of the tablet-catching apparatus on the down platform, while the empty bicycle rack adjacent to the signal box is symptomatic of the air of decay that, in the following months, will inevitably transform the scene of what was once the heart of this rural market town. *Tim Chapman*

Left On 1 January 1966, under the admiring gaze of two boys in the field, No 35011 General Steam Navigation arrives at Stalbridge with the LCGB 'Mendip Merchantman' special at 12.10, some 20 minutes behind schedule. Its late running had held up the 09.50 service from Bath to Bournemouth, headed by very run-down Standard Class 5 No 73001, seen in the station, which had been waiting for some minutes to enter the single line southwards. No 35011 is currently based at Sellindge in Kent and is the subject of an ambitious preservation project that hopes to restore the locomotive to its original 'air-smoothed' condition. *Mark Warburton, courtesy of Mrs Margaret Warburton*

The green sign propped up on the platform indicating that this is Sturminster Newton would surely command a high price today amongst collectors, but proved just too large to liberate for one dependent upon public transport! Track had only just been removed from the station area at the time of this July 1967 picture, the railhead being at the River Stour crossing a short distance to the north.

Above Shillingstone station basks in the summer sun of a July day in 1967. Track removal reached this location shortly before this date and odd lengths of rail still lie around the site. The red board for fire buckets, with its hooks in place, can be seen on the right. This is the only Dorset Central station to survive to the present day and is currently the subject of a restoration project that has seen the station building restored, the signal box re-erected and track laid through the platforms.

Inset This unusual view looking north at Shillingstone, taken in April 1966 shortly after closure, shows the southern end of the passing loop where the line becomes single track on to Blandford. A film of rust coats the rails and the post to the left will no longer be required to inform crews of the gradient change. Note the presence of concrete sleepers. *Tim Chapman*

THE SOMERSET & DORSET LINE

Right Although closed in 1956, Stourpaine & Durweston Halt shows few signs of dereliction some eleven years on in 1967. Custody of the signboard from here, which still exists, was the subject of a regular cricket match between the two villages mentioned in the station's title, although willingness to relinquish safekeeping by the losers is not always apparent, I understand. The sign is nowadays preserved in the wall of a children's playground adjacent to Durweston First School.

Below right Blandford Forum station shows some evidence, in the goods yard behind the signal box, of goods traffic being carried in the summer of 1967. However, the only regular items by this time comprised coal and fertiliser, with some hops for the local brewery. All this could be carried comfortably by one or two trains per week. Note the interesting survival of the platform-end water crane complete with bag.

Memories of happier times at Blandford are recalled by this view of 9F No 92209 halted with the Southern Counties Touring Society special the 'South Western Rambler' of 8 March 1964. The tour had started from Waterloo with 'Britannia' 'Pacific' No 70020 Mercury in charge as far as Salisbury, where the 2-10-0 took over for the run to Bournemouth via Templecombe.

The Somerset & Dorset Line

Above How things have changed two years on in this scene of the SLS last-day special photographed in a similar position at Blandford Forum with Nos 48706 and 80043 in charge. *Mark Warburton, courtesy of Mrs Margaret Warburton*

Right The southbound special is seen again as a northbound working headed by 'Merchant Navy' 'Pacific' No 35028 Clan Line is about to enter the station. For a short time both trains were present, enabling photographs to be taken of this unique event. *Mark Warburton, courtesy of Mrs Margaret Warburton*

Cole to Blandford Forum

LAST TRAIN TO BLANDFORD

Following withdrawal of regular S&D line passenger services in March 1966, Blandford Forum continued to see freight traffic until January 1969, when final closure came. The handful of passenger specials that traversed the route from Broadstone Junction to the Georgian market town during this period are recalled here.

As darkness fell on the evening of Saturday 5 March 1966 the final scheduled passenger services left Blandford Forum station on the Somerset & Dorset line. By this time the infamous interim 'Emergency Service' was in operation, consisting of just a handful of trains in each direction. The last northward service was the 19.34 to Bath Green Park, which was so delayed by 'last rites' and the number of passengers wishing to travel that it reached Bath some 50 minutes late. The final southbound departure was the 21.39 to Bournemouth Central, the traditional S&D terminus of Bournemouth West having been closed six months previously. Additionally there had been two enthusiast specials operated by the LCGB and the GWS, the former passing through Blandford just before 18.00, unforgettably hauled by two unrebuilt Bulleid 'Pacifics'. The following day there were a couple of specials, there being no Sunday service on the S&D, the first heading northwards and making a 5-minute stop at Blandford at about 13.30, crossing with the southbound special, the final northbound return leg reaching the Georgian market town just before 17.00. And that should have been it as far as passengers were concerned, as there remained merely a freight service southwards to Broadstone Junction.

Although not known at the time, the LCGB tour illustrated here was to be the final passenger train to operate from Blandford a couple of months before complete closure of the remaining freight-only stub of the former S&D main line. Following closure to regular passenger trains on 6 March 1966, Blandford was to see a handful of passenger specials over the next 2¾ years. The first reappearance of coaching stock was on 21 May, barely two months after formal closure, when Standard Class 3 No 77014 was seen with a British Young Traveller Society special. Arriving at Blandford's up platform, rather than the down, which was officially the only one in use at this time, No 77014 had to run round its four-coach train to work tender-first back to Broadstone.

A few weeks later, on 6 July, No 34012 Launceston had charge of a nine-coach special for workers at the local brewery of Hall & Woodhouse. The destination was Brighton. Brewing of beer had been a local industry since 1777, when an enterprising Charles Hall started brewing for the troops that were stationed in Weymouth to counter the growing French threat across the Channel. The brewery is currently owned by the seventh generation of the Woodhouse family, and there had been a long tradition of organising an outing by rail for the workforce. The company's final rail outing was scheduled for 15 June 1968, but

Displaying headcode 1Z13, green-liveried Brush Type 4 No D1986 prepares to leave Blandford with the last ever passenger train, the LCGB 'Hampshireman' special of 3 November 1968. A few weeks later Blandford lost its surviving freight service, and 105 years after the opening of the station in September 1863 it ceased to be a railway-served town. No D1986, introduced to traffic in January 1966, was scrapped in November 1999.

This last passenger train to arrive at Blandford was headed up the remaining stub of the line from Broadstone Junction by electro-diesel No E6108, with No D1986 at the rear of the train for the return journey.

this time, following the end of steam on the SR on 9 July 1967, the train was diesel-hauled by 'Crompton' No D6540. The destination was Kew, but as arrival back in Poole was at night the special was barred from returning to Blandford, so passengers had to board road coaches to finish their trip.

Between these brewery excursions another couple of enthusiasts' specials were operated, the first being on 16 October 1966. This was topped and tailed by Standards Nos 77014 with 76026 hauling the LCGB special 'The Dorset & Hants' rail tour. I vividly recall watching this pass at Bailey Gate crossing on the A31, where a long tailback of cars was hampered by numerous parked vehicles, their occupants eager to see the passing spectacle of five coaches and two locomotives. No 76026 was at the front for the journey to Blandford, while No 77014 led on the return journey as far as Poole, where the train reversed for a trip down the Hamworthy Goods line. The tour had previously visited the Ringwood line with the two Standards.

The second rail tour involved Ivatt tank No 41320, which worked the 'Hants & Dorset Branch Flyer'. This was billed as the last steam-hauled tour over the Blandford line, which, with the end of SR steam fast approaching, proved to be the case. Originating at Southampton, the tour began with 'USA' haulage in the shape of No 30064 to Fawley, being relieved at Totton on the return by No 80151, which took a trip down the Lymington branch. On return to Brockenhurst the tour recommenced with the Ivatt in charge for a trip up to Blandford and return, followed by an outing on the Swanage branch.

The last passenger train to arrive at Blandford was headed by Class 74 electro-diesel No E6108 with Brush Type 4 (Class 47) No D1986 at the rear of the train for the return journey. The train was the LCGB 'Hampshireman' special of 3 November 1968, which was scheduled to depart from Blandford at 16.15 following a 20-minute stop. The Class 74 had headed the train on the outgoing run, which had started from Waterloo that morning and proceeded via Guildford and Cosham to Fareham, where No D6506 took over for a trip on the Gosport branch, followed by a visit to the Fawley branch. On arrival back at Totton, No E6108 took over for the run to Poole, where it was joined on the rear by No D1986. Following a foray up the Blandford stub, D1986 assumed sole charge for the return to Waterloo via Alresford and Ascot. This had not been the first appearance of a Class 74 on the line, for in April/May 1968 one had been noted on the freight service to Bailey Gate on at least two occasions. However, this was probably the first time that the class had penetrated as far as Blandford. Displaying headcode 1Z13, green-liveried No D1986 left Blandford with the last ever passenger service, with E6108 this time on the rear. A few weeks later Blandford lost its surviving freight service and, 105 years after the opening of the station in September 1863, it ceased to be a railway-served town. No E6108 was withdrawn in December 1977, with No D1986, introduced to traffic in January 1966, following in November 1999.

THE SOMERSET & DORSET LINE

CHARLTON MARSHALL TO BOURNEMOUTH WEST

Left **Charlton Marshall Halt** illustrates the stages of track removal, with the former up line reduced to ranks of sleepers adjacent to the platform, while in the distance they still retain their chairs. Both concrete Southern-style nameboards survive in this view taken a few weeks before goods traffic from Blandford ceased in January 1969.

Below left **Spetisbury** was opened in 1860 but following reduction to unstaffed status in 1934 closed prematurely in 1956. The buildings were demolished in the early 1960s but in this view a single track was still serving Blandford for goods traffic. This facility lasted for nearly three years after closure of the S&D to passengers in 1966.

Above 'Bailey Gate for Sturminster Marshall' proclaims the station sign in this view taken during the Blandford line's freight-only existence in 1968. Only one line is in use to judge from the relative condition of the two tracks. Today the site is lost beneath a roundabout and road serving an industrial estate.

Inset Track was removed from Bailey Gate in May 1970 and many lengths of rail can be seen, with chairs still attached, lying on the platform. The creamery in the background appears to be going strong, but even this fell on hard times and changed ownership subsequently. The platforms were not removed until 1988.

Right Just after 5.00pm on 18 September 1960 S&D 7F No 53804 draws to a halt at Bailey Gate with the LCGB 'South Western Limited' rail tour. It had brought the tour, which started from London's Cannon Street station, up from Broadstone Junction. It would proceed as far as Salisbury via Templecombe, where it would hand over to a 'T9' for the return to London Waterloo.

Left Bailey Gate signal box, seen here in April 1968 during its period of demotion to ground frame status, controlled access to the adjacent creamery sidings. By the summer of that year milk traffic was spasmodic, and by the following January all trains had ceased to run. The box was demolished in 1970.

THE SOMERSET & DORSET LINE

Above **Corfe Mullen Halt**, situated on the single line between Corfe Mullen Junction and Broadstone, was opened in 1928 together with three other halts to try and tap local traffic, but it was to survive just twenty-eight years before closure in 1956. The deep cutting here was infilled after closure of the line and the halt simply buried.

Left The gates and box are still in place at Bailey Gate crossing, initially downgraded to a ground frame but since May 1968 closed completely, Blandford goods train crews having to operate the gates manually. It is readily apparent that only the down line is still in use by late 1968. The wooden portion of the box was demolished in 1970, but the brick base and house lasted into the 1990s, although they have since been replaced by a bungalow.

Broadstone Junction is still essentially complete, albeit with amputated signal arms on the gantry controlling the divergence of the S&D route to the left and the former LSWR 'Old Road' to West Moors straight ahead. Tablet-exchanging apparatus still looks to be in place outside the junction box, as is the 20mph speed restriction sign.

CHARLTON MARSHALL TO BOURNEMOUTH WEST

Broadstone Junction still retains track to all four platforms in this 1972 view. By this date, however, goods traffic to Blandford had ceased and only oil to West Moors and goods to Wimborne were still carried.

Left **Creekmoor Halt on the Bournemouth-Ringwood-Brockenhurst 'Old Road' was also served by S&D trains. It was a typical Southern concrete construction and is seen here during the period when goods services still operated to Wimborne. This traffic ceased in 1977.**

Below left **Only the boarded-up ground floor windows belie the fact that this is a functioning terminus. However, it has been more than two years since Bournemouth West was first partially, then, in September 1965, totally closed and services diverted to the Central station. A fine array of classic cars of the period adorns the forecourt including a Hillman Minx, VW Beetle and Vauxhall Viva.**

'Battle of Britain' 'Pacific' No 34051 Winston Churchill is seen at Bournemouth West station, the traditional terminus for S&D trains, with photographers thronging the tracks. It will shortly take out the LCGB 'Wessex Downsman Rail Tour' on its return to Waterloo. This tour ran on two dates in 1965, 4 April and 2 May, and on both occasions this 'Pacific' handled the return leg from Bournemouth.

Above The turntable at nearby Bournemouth Central shed plays host to No 48706, which, together with No 80043, has brought in the SLS special of Sunday 6 March 1966. *Mark Warburton, courtesy of Mrs Margaret Warburton*

Top left Although a rake of coaches lies in one of the platform roads to the right, the main tracks have already been lifted in this view of Bournemouth West station, closed to passengers temporarily in August 1965 with total closure following a few weeks later on 4 October. S&D trains were diverted to Central station or terminated inconveniently at Parkstone. Most of the track was lifted in the area of West station in October 1965.

Bottom left This platform-end view of the empty terminus building shows the majority of tracks removed, with just one siding still serving a platform at the far left. In the distance can be seen an EMU near the carriage washing plant, the nearest that electric traction came to Bournemouth West. Note the 'Refreshments' sign still hanging forlornly from the roofing girders.

THE SOMERSET & DORSET LINE

50TH ANNIVERSARY CELEBRATIONS

Left The SDRHT based at Midsomer Norton had hoped to have a Standard Class 4 tank masquerading as No 80043, which operated on the last day of normal services, Saturday 5 March 1966, but unfortunately one was not available. However, the Trust did manage to produce 'Jinty' No 47406, representing a class that was used right up to the end of operations in March 1966 on banking duties and for shunting at Writhlington Colliery. The 0-6-0T, currently resident on the Great Central Railway, is seen here at the beautifully restored Midsomer Norton station on Saturday 5 March 2016, exactly fifty years to the day since the last service train ran through.

50TH ANNIVERSARY CELEBRATIONS

Opposite below **The Trust's recently refurbished Sentinel, examples of which design operated at nearby Radstock in former times, was also in steam and attracted the attention of the visitors.**

This page and following page **However, the SDRHT did manage to recreate the last weekend atmosphere on 10th and 11th. September 2016 when Standard tank No. 80072 from the Llangollen Railway assumed the guise of both 80041 and 80043, the locomotives which double headed the final northbound service from Templecombe to Bath 50 years ago.**
All Peter Russell

REMEMBERING
THE
RAILWAY
50 Years Since Closure of
the Somerset & Dorset Line
5 MAR 16
Evercreech Village Hall Admit One - £2

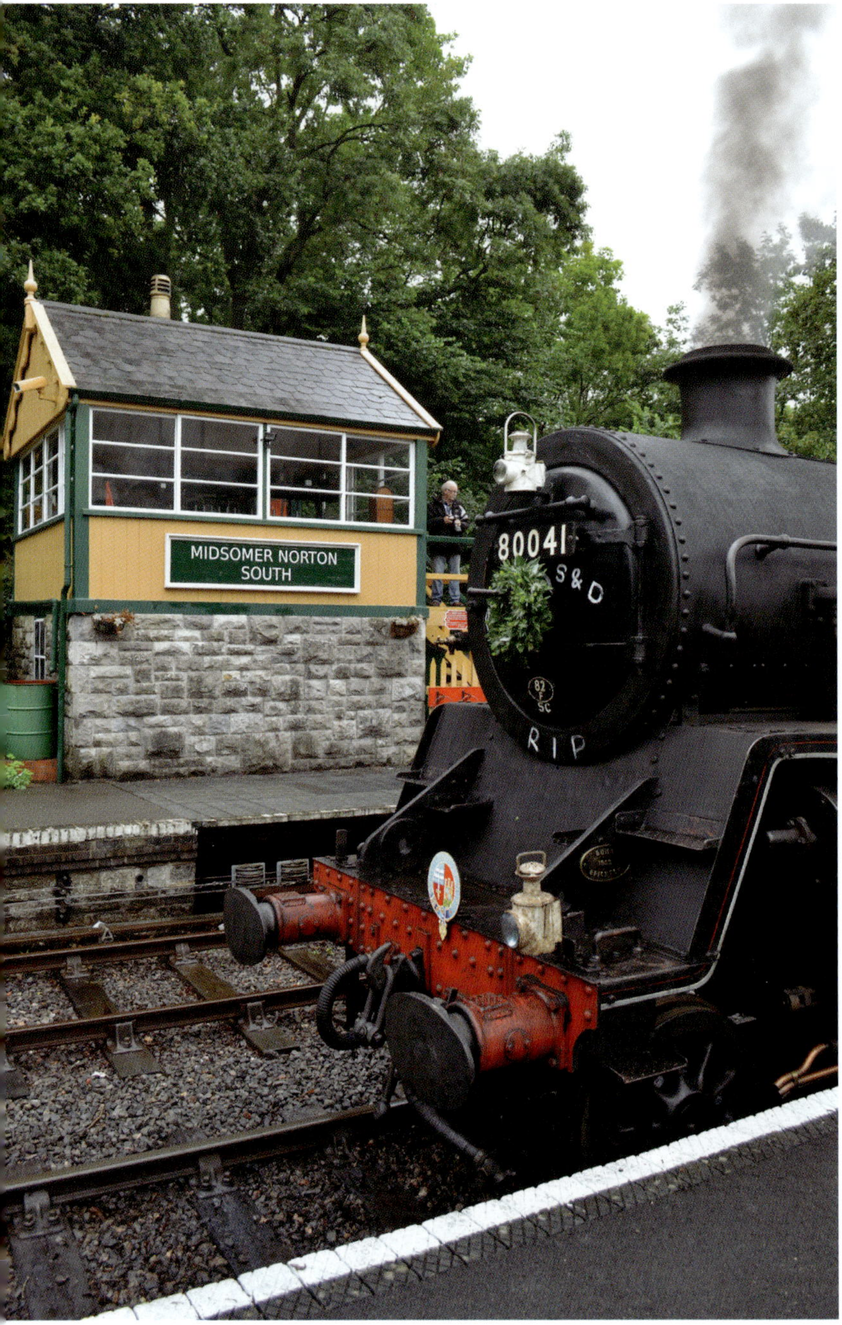

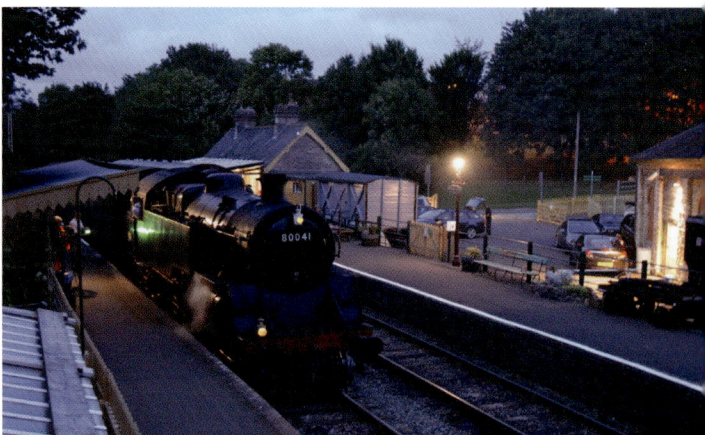

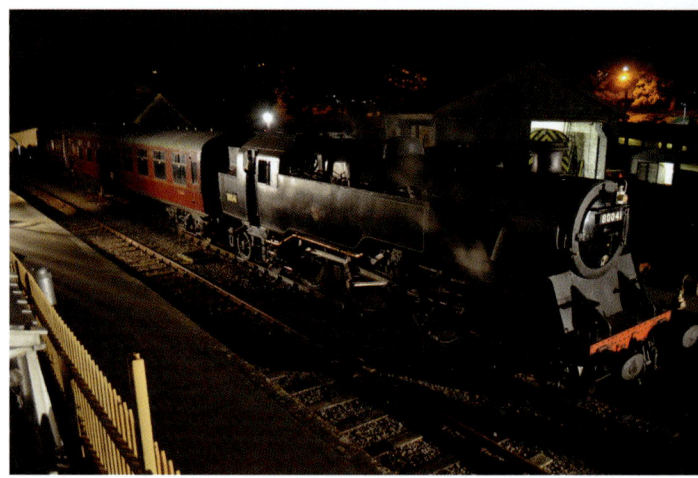

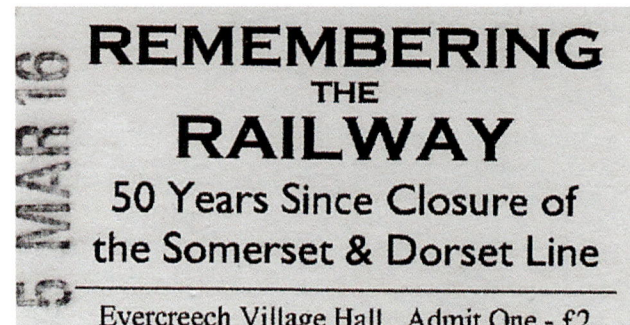

50TH ANNIVERSARY CELEBRATIONS

Above and right A re-enactment of Bath Tramways rail replacement service No B56A, subsequently renumbered 178, which originally ran from Bath to Cole, was captured at Cole. The vehicle is 981 EHY, a Bristol MW saloon in Bath Services livery, which entered service with Bristol Omnibus in 1959 and operated until withdrawal in 1975. Passing through three further owners, it was acquired by the Bristol Omnibus Vehicle Collection in 2011. It is seen parked at Cole Station while operating between there and Evercreech on 5 March 2016; the rear of the station building, now a private house, is visible in the background of the lower picture. The original rail replacement service in 1966 provided just two journeys, primarily for schoolchildren, between these two points, as can be seen from the accompanying timetable.

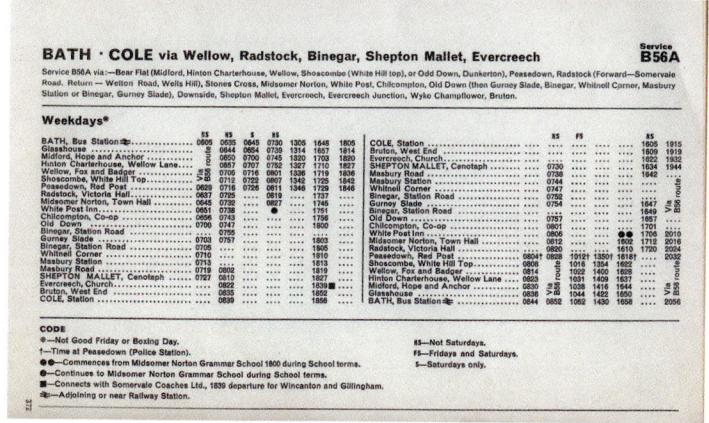

123

Opposite **The West Somerset Railway's Somerset & Dorset Gala of March 2016 featured several locomotive types associated with the S&D. Perhaps two of the most tangible artefacts of the old S&D are the pair of preserved Fowler 7Fs, Nos 53808 and 53809. During the S&D Gala both locomotives were working, and No 53809 is seen departing from Crowcombe for Minehead in double harness with 4F No 44422, another type long associated with the old line.**

Right **No 53808 had recently emerged from overhaul and was captured at Bishops Lydeard, which had assumed the mantle of Templecombe for the event, sporting an 82F (Bath Green Park) shedplate and a typical reporting number, M227.**

Below **Coming in to Crowcombe station, masquerading as Shepton Mallet, is a reincarnation of Standard tank No 80043, which as mentioned above was a key player in the last day of service trains fifty years before. This is in fact No 80072, normally based at the Llangollen Railway.**

The two Bulleid 'Pacifics', Nos 34006 Bude and 34057 Biggin Hill, come to rest under the impressive overall roof of Green Park station in Bath just after 3.00pm on 5 March 1966, having brought in the LCGB special. Note one of the loco crew trimming the coal on the tender of the leading engine. Just over an hour later the pair would depart from Bath for a last run to Bournemouth. *Mark Warburton, courtesy of Mrs Margaret Warburton.*

INDEX

Ashcott & Meare 72

Bailey Gate 109-111
Bailey Gate crossing 112
Bason Bridge.. 73-75
Bath Green Park 6-13,126
Binegar 42-43
Bishops Lydeard 125
Blandford Forum 100-107
Broadstone 114-115
Bournemouth Central 119
Bournemouth West 116-118
Burnham-on-Sea 84-85

Cemetary Lane Crossing 68
Charlton Marshall 108
Chilcompton 40
Cock Mill crossing 67
Cole 86-87,123
Combe Down Tunnel 15-16,128
Corfe Mullen... 113
Creekmoor.. 116
Crowcombe 124-125

Devonshire Tunnel/bank 14

Evercreech Junction................................... 5,52-65
Evercreech New 52

Glastonbury & Street 69-70

Henstridge 94
Highbridge 75-80,83-84
Highbridge Works 78,81-82

Kilmersdon Colliery 33-34

Lyncombe Vale... 14
Masbury 44-47
Midford.. 17-19

Midsomer Norton South 1,38-40,120-122
Moorewood.. 41

Polsham 72
Pylle 66

Radstock North................................... 24-29,35-37
Radstock West 30-32
River Brue aqueduct bridge............................... 3

Stalbridge 95-96
Shepton Mallet Charlton Road 47-51
Shepton Mallet High Street 51
Shillingstone 99
Shoscombe & Single Hill 21
Somervale Coaches 71
Spetisbury.. 108
Stalbridge 95-96
Stourpaine & Durweston 100
Sturminster Newton 97-98

Templecombe 88-93

Wellow 20
West Pennard 67
Wincanton 88
Writhlington Colliery 22-23

Next page **Combe Down cameo. Framed by the north portal of Combe Down tunnel the permanent way curves away on a falling gradient of 1 in 50 towards Bath Junction. At this date, November 1967, the line only played host to the occasional track removal train and it was to be only a matter of weeks before these too had passed into history. Today one can walk or cycle through the tunnel which re-opened as part of the Two Tunnels project in 2013.**